# A Gift for You

PRESENTED TO

_____

BY

_____

DATE

_____

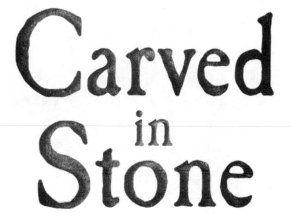

# Carved in Stone

*Exploring the*
**TEN COMMANDMENTS**
*with your children*

## By Craig Peters
*Illustrated by Sharon Frank Mazgaj*

# Carved in Stone

ISBN 0-9715840-0-1

For additional copies of this book visit
your local bookstore or contact:

SAFE HARBOR PRESS
3222 Robin's Trace
Akron, OH 44319

Carlisle Printing
WALNUT CREEK

2673 TR 421
Sugarcreek, OH 44681

# Dedication

To my loving wife Ann, who gave me the idea, and to my children Amanda, Nicole, and Jared who constantly asked, "Daddy, please tell us one more story."

# Contents

# *Introduction*

## Caught Up In The Moment

Nothing so deeply captures the heart and remains in a child's memory as a story. As long as children are willing to dream and imagine, there will be stories, and as long as there are those who are willing to crawl back into the world of childhood there will be stories.

To enter into and hold the mind of a child or young person is one of the hardest of all writers' tasks. For with the art of story writing must also come the art of story telling, where the senses are explored and imagination runs free. Truly, a good story is like a good friend. We never grow tired of seeing the same faces, or hearing the same words which so easily are unfolded and etched in the innocent mind of the young listener or reader. When a good story is told it literally lifts the person mentally from their current setting and places them in another dimension of time which will have an effect on them for years to come. I know, because it's happened to me and continues to happen. As an adult, I find story telling an escape from the cynicism and cruelty of this world. Making up stories and telling them takes me to a better place where life is simpler, offering more joy, laughter, love, and suspense than this darkened world in which I reside.

I've seen children caught up in the moment of a story. I have three children of my own. I've seen the look of amazement in their eyes or the sparkle of life when a story brings hope and value. At a campfire, story hour, or at bedtime, I've seen hundreds of children be captivated by something good and wholesome and priceless.

*Carved In Stone* is a collection of ten short stories I have written to bring out the biblical truths of the Ten Commandments in a way that will be understandable and relevant for children. Just try to explain to a child about adultery (Commandment 7) or making no false idol before God (Commandment 2) and you will see a multitude of blank stares looking back at you. But put them in a modern day story and, "voila," they get the message and they will plead to hear "just one more."

My heartfelt desire as you read these stories to your children, or as you yourself snuggle under a warm blanket, is that in some way you will be caught up in the moment and become not only children again, but children of God. May these stories reflect the principles of God's Word which were carved in stone thousands of years ago, and be carved on our hearts today and for generations to come.

# The King's Favor

**T**he mood in the Kingdom was contagious. People smiled at one another as they bought and sold items in the marketplace. Dogs were playing, children were joyfully singing, and if you listened closely, you could hear the people whispering.

"They say he's coming home tonight," said a young man.

"He's been gone for so long," replied an older woman.

"I feel safer when he's home," a little girl said as she clung to her mother's leg.

The Kingdom was absolutely beautiful. During the day when the sun was overhead, the King's palace sparkled with a colorful array of lights. At night the palace lights lit up the sky giving the weary or lost traveler a point of reference to find their way home. Just looking at it gave a person goose bumps.

People continued to rush around as they got ready for the

homecoming of the King. You see, the King had been away on a long trip, traveling to other foreign lands to meet with other important kings and queens. But as exciting as this was, the King would tell you there was no Kingdom like his Kingdom, and no better people than his people. He always looked forward to the warm greeting he would receive when he came through the gate of the Kingdom.

Several days after the King returned, he would always stand before his entire Kingdom and treat his people like royalty. In return, the people would offer to their King a song, and shout in celebration of his safe return.

Strangely enough however, there were several individuals who were always the first to see the King, even before the Queen or his servants. They were the most unlikely subjects one would ever think of greeting the King when he came home.

You see, just inside the Kingdom gate lived four beggars. They were poor, dirty, and smelled like the local garbage dump that they visited daily in order to find food to survive.

The beggars were seen as unimportant and useless to those who lived in the Kingdom.

"They're useless," people would mock.

"Why them pigs smell better than them beggars," said others as they laughed and walked on by.

But not to the King!

You see, when the King's carriage came through the gate, the beggars were the first of his people whom he would see. And he would always stop to greet them. Graciously he would offer the beggars bread, nuts, and fruit that he had received as gifts from other kingdoms far away. You would think they would be grateful for the King's act of love and concern, but instead they were rude and disrespectful toward the King. They scoffed and carried on, showing no sign of loyalty or allegiance to the King of the Kingdom.

"When are you going to take care of us?" yelled an old-timer who hardly had any teeth.

"You're no King! You only take care of yourself!" jeered another lad who kept pulling on his pants so they wouldn't fall down.

"How about trading places for awhile," said another who was so drunk he was barely able to stand up.

This saddened the King and he hoped that one day they would understand.

> *What do we learn about the King in the story?*
>
> *What do we learn about the beggars?*

If you could look deep into the heart of the King you would find that the true reason for his stopping at the gate was not for these ungrateful beggars, but for another beggar named Melvin.

Melvin was a simple man. He lived by himself in a tiny shack right beside the stone wall that protected the Kingdom from the enemy. His shack was dark and damp, and when it rained, which was often, the water would drip down the wall and into his home making his dirt floor nothing more than a mud hole. As you entered the shack, it gave off a strong odor of garbage, mildew and sweat. Melvin was often found sitting on the dirt floor dressed in tattered clothes that others in the Kingdom had discarded in the local dump. His pants were ripped above the knee and stained with what looked to be last night's meal. His hair was unkempt, his eyes blood shot, and his body ached from having to lay on the dirt floor which was his bed. For years Melvin survived the scorching heat during the summers and somehow withstood the cold desert evenings, the kind where you can see your breath, and you'd give anything for an extra blanket. But Melvin had nothing to give, nothing except a heart of praise for his King. You see, he loved the King dearly. He spoke highly of him to the other beggars and always showed the deepest respect for him when he would come through the gate.

As the sun began to drop below the horizon, Melvin heard a welcoming sound in the distance. He cupped his hand over his ear and, sure enough, he could faintly hear it. The sound of a trumpet in the distance proclaimed the arrival of the King.

Scrambling out of his shack, he brushed himself off and made himself look as presentable as possible. The grin on his face said it all. He was going to see the King. He had looked forward to this day for months, for what would be only a brief moment when he would look at the King and with great honor and loyalty say, "Welcome home– enter into thy Kingdom."

By the time he could see the King's carriage, it was almost dark. Yet he waited patiently in front of the gate. The other beggars refused to come out.

"Only if the King brings us food, will we have a reason to greet him," they said.

But for Melvin the greeting was the part he loved the most. When the gate creaked open and the carriage slowly crossed over into the Kingdom, Melvin would hold out his arms, drop to his knees, and bow his head in honor and respect for his King.

On this grand occasion, Melvin made sure he had his torn jacket that he used as a pillow at night. Oh, he knew it was no red carpet, but certainly the King deserved a royal welcome when he arrived. So he would throw the jacket on the ground as a royal welcome. Then came that special moment when their eyes met. The King of honor and power looking straight into the eyes of a weak and powerless beggar.

They smiled at each other before a word was spoken. They both longed for this moment when a mere exchanging of words was secondary to a King's heart that was won over by a beggar and a beggar's heart won over by a King.

Melvin, still on his knees, raised his arms toward the King and then toward the Kingdom and shouted, "Welcome home– enter into thy Kingdom!"

The King nodded and motioned Melvin over to him. He spoke tenderly.

"I have missed you."

It was only a few words, but these words are what kept Melvin going. It put hope into Melvin's heart. The hope to survive, to never give up, to always believe. It was these words that caused Melvin to realize that nothing could ever separate or take the place of the love he held for the King.

Weeks went by. The King and his people had settled back into the routine of the Kingdom. But something was wrong with the King. His mind was on something heavy.

"What is it, my King?" asked the Queen.

He said it was nothing. But she knew better. For hours he would sit on his royal throne thinking and reasoning over something that only he could picture. Walking the royal palace late at night, unable to sleep, unable to eat. Until finally the day came when he made his decision.

He called for one of his trusted servants, Limar.

"Limar," said the King, "I have an important task for you. You mustn't tell anyone."

"Yes my Lord," said Limar.

"Tonight I want you to wear some of my finest kingly clothes. I want you to dress like royalty."

"What for, my Lord?" asked Limar hoping he had not crossed a line in questioning the King.

"Tonight I want you to take one of my finest horses, go out the back gate and ride out into the country. After one hour, I want you to ride back to the palace, but I want you to go to the front gate where you will find four beggars. Acting as if you are a powerful King from a foreign land, tell them that one day you will be king of this Kingdom; and this will all be yours. And then give them these."

The King held out four small bags filled with gold and silver coins.

"My Lord," gasped Limar, "there is more here than one receives in six months wages.

"I know," replied the King.

"Tell the beggars that when you become king everyone including them will live better and will no longer have to live by the gate and scavenge for food in the local dump. The Kingdom will be different because there will soon be a new king. Then show them the bags of coins and tell them that these are theirs as long as, when the time comes, they show their loyalty and devotion to you and not to the present King."

Limar agreed without asking any more questions.

That night the clouds rolled in and it rained harder than anyone in the Kingdom could ever remember.

"Limar could be trusted," thought the King, "even under these heavy rains, he will be loyal."

Riding one of the King's finest horses, Limar rode up to the front gate.

"Anyone there?" shouted Limar under the heavy rain.

Moments later, out came four beggars. Limar told them exactly what the King had told him. When he pulled out the bags filled with coins, and gave them to the beggars, their eyes widened as they began to laugh and then dance in the rain.

"You may have these coins to use as you wish," said Limar, "but you must remember that when it is time to appoint a new king you must be loyal to me and not to the present king. Is that understood?"

"Sure, not a problem."

"You got it."

"Sounds like a deal," replied three of the beggars before they took off into the night to squander their wealth.

Melvin, however, just stood there with the bag of coins in his hand. "How could I do such a thing," he thought. "How could I trade away the love I have for the King for a few coins which will be used up and forgotten years from now?"

"I cannot take this," said Melvin handing the coins back to Limar.

"My heart is with the King and always will be. You could give me all the riches of the Kingdom and it will not change my mind. Nothing or no one will come before the devotion that I have to my King."

"Very well," said Limar as he mounted his horse and left the way he came. Soon afterwards, he circled around and came into the back gate giving the news to the King.

*What do we learn about Melvin that tells us the way he feels and lives for the King?*

*How can people tell if God is first in your life?*

Shortly after midnight the King secretly dressed in beggars clothes and slipped out of the royal palace. The rain was still falling heavily when the King walked through the marketplace and on toward the front gate.

Melvin's shack had so much rain coming into it, that it was nothing more than a huge mud puddle. Melvin now huddled in one of the corners trying to stay warm with his tattered jacket tightly wrapped around him. Suddenly, he heard a knock at the door. Melvin opened the door to see a beggar whom he had not seen before. The man looked just as poor and dirty as he. Melvin had a hard time seeing the stranger's face because the rain was falling so hard.

"Come with me," said the stranger to Melvin. "I have found shelter for us."

Quickly, Melvin and the stranger made their way through the muddy streets. Melvin kept his face down, for the rain was falling so hard that it would sting his face if he looked up.

Moments later the stranger in front of him stopped. Melvin raised his head to see that he was standing in front of the King's palace. It was breathtaking. The lights and beauty of the palace lit up the night. It was a picture of heaven, Melvin thought. He felt the goose bumps appear on his arms.

The stranger came over and stood before Melvin. Suddenly he did something that surprised Melvin. Dropping to his knees, the stranger spread out his arms. His face now appeared having been illuminated by the light of the palace. To Melvin's amaze-

ment, there on his knees with outstretched arms was the King!

Smiling, the King shouted, "Welcome home my friend– enter into thy Kingdom," and they walked into the King's palace together– forever.

*Melvin found favor in the eyes of the King.*

*In what ways should we make God first so we will find favor with our God and King?*

## The First Commandment

EXODUS 20:3

### You shall have no other gods before me.

(Put God first in your life)

# Scripture Readings

*But seek first His kingdom and His righteousness,
and all these things will be given to you as well.*

MATTHEW 6:33

*Show proper respect to everyone: Love the brotherhood
of believers, fear God, honor the king.*

1 PETER 2:17

## KEY THOUGHT –

*When you always put God first you never have
to worry about Him being last!*

# The Guessing Game

Max and Missy crawled up onto the bed and snuggled close to their father. Even after a long day the children could still smell the familiar aftershave that he put on each morning before he left for work. Pulling the children close and giving them a little squeeze and kiss on the forehead, the children slid under the covers and propped up their pillows in anticipation of another one of Father's exciting bedtime stories. Tonight however, Father did not have a book on his lap like he usually did. Instead he held a small box about the size of a shoe box with the number two written on the lid.

"What's in the box?" said Max.

"Is it two kittens?" asked Missy as she touched it with caution.

"I bet it's a two-headed snake," hissed Max as Missy quickly withdrew her hand.

Father laughed, "Well, I can promise you one thing," he said, "it's not two kittens and it's certainly not a two-headed snake. Tonight, we are going to play the guessing game."

"How do we play?" asked the children.

"Well," smiled Father, "you need to tell me what's in the box and then explain to me what the object in the box has to do with the number two."

"How are we going to do that?" inquired Max.

"Both of you working together can ask as many questions as you can think of until you guess the object or until you need a little hint."

"Like, is the object in the box red?" said Missy.

"Exactly," said Father.

"This sounds like fun," said Max, now sitting up on his knees so he would not miss anything.

"Okay, ladies first," declared Missy as she flipped her strawberry colored hair over her shoulders. "Is there only one item in the box?"

"Yes," replied Father.

"Okay, now its my turn," smiled Max. Max sat in silence for what seemed like forever, thinking over what his question might be.

"Sometime today before we all grow old," said Missy rolling her eyes.

Finally Max said, "Is the object alive?"

"No," said Father.

Missy folded her arms and had a serious look on her face. "Is the object blue?" she asked.

"Yes, some of it," replied Father.

Max scratched his head, and finally said, "Can you eat this object?"

"I wouldn't recommend it," smiled Father.

"Is the object soft and cuddly like my teddy bear?" said Missy.

"No it's not soft and cuddly," said Father, "but you sure are." He pulled her close, smelling her freshly washed hair from their evening bath.

Max was deep in thought as he rubbed his chin. "Is it made out of wood?"

"Yes," said Father.

Max and Missy shouted together. . . "Yessss" as they giggled, and grew with excitement over getting their first solid clue to what was in the box.

"Okay," said Father, "we know that the object is made of wood and some of it's blue."

"It's a canoe!!" Max said without thinking.

"A canoe?" laughed Missy and her dad. Max suddenly realized what he had just said and laughed so hard he almost fell off the bed.

"Is the object in the box green?" asked Missy.

"Yes," said Father as his eyes widened realizing the children were inching closer to the answer.

"Is there anything carved in the wood?" asked Max.

"As a matter of fact, there certainly is," said Father.

By now Max and Missy could hardly contain themselves.

After several more guesses Max and Missy began struggling to come up with questions as to what was in the box before them. But they also had to figure out what the number two had to do with what was in the box. This was harder than they thought. Father could tell they needed help.

"Who needs a hint?" asked Father

Both hands immediately went up.

"Do you remember when we drove out to Arizona last year for our family vacation?" asked Father. Both children nodded. "What were some of the places we visited when we were there?"

"We visited Grandma," said Missy.

"And we went to the Grand Canyon" said Max

"Was there anywhere else we stopped?" Their dad was now holding up his hand and saying, "How," like a brave Indian warrior.

Max and Missy shouted, "The Navajo gift shop on the Indian reservation!"

"Right!" exclaimed Dad. Do you remember buying anything in the Navajo gift shop that might be small enough to fit into this box?"

Missy and Max sat in silence. "I remember Mom bought an Indian blanket and a pair of Indian moccasins," said Missy.

"I bought a drum to play with in the car," said Max.

"How could we ever forget," said Missy and Father as they both covered their ears with their hands. "It was so loud."

"Do you remember what daddy bought?"

Immediately the children knew what was in the box.

Together they yelled, "a Totem Pole."

"Right," said Dad.

He lifted up the lid and there was a small wooden carving of a Totem Pole. He took it out of the box to show the children. Colors of blue, green, red, and yellow covered the surface of the totem pole. Carved on the pole were three animals of the wilderness. On the top of the pole was carved an eagle, a symbol of leadership and courage to the Navajo Indians. In the middle a bear was carved, a symbol of strength and protection, the bear protects and defends his cubs from harm. Finally, at the bottom of the Totem Pole, was a carving of a beaver, a symbol of resourcefulness and hard labor, representing the end-less hours building a strong home for itself and family. Max and Missy both took turns holding the Totem Pole and mar-veled over the beauty of the carved object.

"Do you remember what the Navajo Indian at the shop told us about the Totem Pole?" asked Father.

"I forget" said both Missy and Max.

"The Indian told us that Totem Poles were carved to give tribute or remembrance to someone or something special, but it was never to be used to worship or be bowed down to."

"I remember now," said Max. He told us that the Totem Pole was to be a symbol of honor, but never to be worshiped or exalted above God."

"That's right," said Dad. "You see, God created the tree to make the Totem Pole. He created the eagle to soar, the bear to protect, and the beaver to build, but none of these things are to ever be more important than God. We worship God Almighty, the creator of heaven and earth, never the creature. We are told as children of God never to exalt or praise graven images or idols.

Only God is to be exalted and praised." Father leaned over and picked up his Bible from the night stand next to his bed. He opened it up and read:

"Come, let us bow down in worship, let us kneel before the Lord our Maker."

"There are some who have ruined the message of the Totem

Pole by seeing and using it as a graven image or idol to be worshipped. This is not right," said Father.

> *What are some things you can think of that*
> *God has created for the sole purpose to draw*
> *people to Him and not to creation?*

Dad looked into the eyes of his children and smiled, "Okay what does the Totem Pole have to do with the number two written on the lid of the box?" Max and Missy smiled.

"That's easy," said Missy, "we've been learning about this in our Sunday School class at church. The number two stands for the second commandment."

"You are correct," said Dad as he gave both of them a high five. The second commandment tells us that we are not to have or make for ourselves any idol in the form of anything in heaven or on earth. We are not to bow down, worship or make anything more important than God."

"That was fun," said Max, as he began to climb out of bed. "Can we play the guessing game again sometime?"

"Not so fast buddy," said Dad, "the lesson isn't over."

"I now have a question for both of you. Is there anything that you have or own that, if not careful, could become an object of worship rather than God?"

Max lowered his head, and quietly said, "I know that the superstar trading cards I share with my friends can become so important to me that sometimes that's all I think about."

"Could that become something that you begin to idolize and worship more than the Creator of all things?" asked Father.

"Yes," admitted Max.

Dad held Max close. "Let's not let that happen, okay buddy?"

"Okay Dad."

"How about you Missy, is there anything that could become an idol and be exalted above God our Creator?" inquired Father. Missy also had her head down.

"Yes," she said.

"What might that be?" asked dad already having a good idea of what she was about to say.

"In my bedroom I have a lot of posters of music groups that I find myself wanting to be like and idolizing."

"Are those posters reminding you of God your Creator or are they causing you to exalt those on the posters?"

Missy looked up with tears in her eyes. "Oh, Daddy, I never thought of it like that before. Would you help me take them down before I go to bed tonight? I don't want anything to ever become more important, or ever take the place of God in my life."

"I would be happy to help you," Dad said as he once again pulled her close.

As Missy and Max crawled into their beds and said their

prayers, they had learned a valuable lesson from the guessing game. Worshiping God and not things, should be the heart of every child who longs to know and be loved by God.

> *Can you think of anything that you own*
> *or is so important to you that it could easily*
> *become an idol of worship?*

# The Second Commandment

EXODUS 20:4

## You shall not make for yourself an idol.

(No person or thing is more important than God)

# Scripture Reading

*For the Lord is the great God, the great King above all gods.
In His hand are the depths of the earth, and the mountain peaks
belong to Him. The sea is His, for He made it, and His hands
formed the dry land. Come, let us bow down in worship, let us
kneel before the Lord our Maker; for He is God and we are the
people of His pasture, the flock under His care.*

PSALM 95:3-7

## KEY THOUGHT –

*Worship the Creator rather than the created.*

# Word Angel

T J. was a good little boy. He always behaved, always listened, and rarely got into trouble. But lately when T.J. came home after school, Mother was beginning to hear words come out of his mouth that were inappropriate.

"T.J.," exclaimed mother, "Where did you pick up this dreadful and disrespectful language? You have never heard words like this in our home before. Where are you picking up these bad words?"

"Oh, I don't think they're bad words," said T.J. "All of my friends who I play with on the playground at school use them all the time. It's like I'm one of the gang when I say the same things," T.J. said with a grin.

"Well you must stop immediately," said mother with a concerned look. "You must be different around these boys and be a good example to them."

"But I can't," said T.J. "They are bigger than me and won't listen to what I have to say."

"You may not be as big as them, but that doesn't mean you have to use the same language as them. I think it would be best if you stayed away from these boys who are using bad language."

"God!" said T.J., "I knew you were going to say that."

"T.J." exclaimed mother. "That is the last time you will use the Lord's name in vain under this roof. Do you understand me?"

As T.J. began to walk away, his mother could hear him use God's name again in a disrespectful way.

T.J.'s mother ran over to him, grabbed his arm and said, "That's enough. The next time you use any of those idle words, you will go straight up to your bedroom."

"Okay, okay, gosh!" muttered T.J. under his breath.

"That's enough," said mother, "up you go!"

"But I was just going out to play football."

"Not today you aren't, you are going to spend time in your room learning the importance of not using bad language."

T.J. slowly walked upstairs and into his room. Mother informed him that he was not allowed to play in his room, or leave his room until dinner was on the table. He could come down when she called and not before. In the meantime she suggested he make things right with God for using His name in vain. So up into bed he went.

Tears began to trickle down his cheeks. "It's not fair," he said to himself as mother closed the door and walked out. Turning over, he buried his head in the pillow and wiped his eyes with a tissue. Before long, T.J. had drifted off to sleep. He dreamed that he was ushered up to the very gates of heaven where an angel greeted him.

"Who are you?" T.J. asked.

"I am the Word Angel," replied the visitor.

"Word Angel? What words are you talking about?"

"The words of heaven," said the angel. "I record every single word that everyone speaks."

"Good Lord," said T.J. without thinking.

"Yes," replied the angel, "that is also written down."

"I'm sorry. I never used to talk like that before, until I started to hang around some of my friends at school."

The angel looked deep into T.J.'s eyes. "Maybe they are not the kind of friends you need in your life."

"What do you mean?" asked T.J.

"Well," said the angel, "God specifically tells us in the third commandment that we are not to take the Lord's name in vain. And maybe if your *friends* are causing you to do this, they aren't really good friends at all. Your friends should bring you closer to God and His love, not further away.

"What does God think about the way I talk?" inquired T.J..

"God is very sad and hurt when someone uses His name in a way that is unkind or in anger. His name is to be used to give Him praise and honor, not dishonor. And when you use His name in vain, you are not giving him honor, but you are being dishonorable. When we use the Lord's name in vain, they become words of death rather than life."

"What do you mean by 'words of death'?"

The angel leaned up against one of the pearly gates and said, "Let's say that every time you said a bad word your tongue turned black and gave off an odor. And what if everyone could see that black tongue? Don't you think it would cause others to stay away from you?"

T.J. nodded as he winced, picturing what that might look like.

"Do you really think you would be playing with those boys on the play ground if every time they spoke a bad word, their tongues got black and their breath became a sour odor?"

"No way," said T.J..

"Well then, why would anyone want to hang around you if you spoke the same words of dishonor to the Lord?"

T.J. never thought how his words could bring hurt and disappointment to God. He did not like the thought of causing God to be sad on account of his words.

"I'm sorry," said T.J.. "I won't say them anymore, and starting today, I will learn to choose my words and my friends more carefully. I will choose friends that speak life, not death."

"Very good. Now there is one more thing you must do," replied the angel.

"What is that?" asked T.J.

"You must apologize to your mother for the way you talked to her and you must apologize to those boys on the playground for the way you have been behaving. Otherwise your word is useless. Do you understand?"

"Yes," replied T.J. with his head down feeling shame and guilt.

"The good news," said the Word Angel, "is that these unholy words in this book can be erased, but only when we ask God to forgive us for our wrongdoing."

"How are the words erased?"

"Your words are erased and cleansed by the blood of our Savior Jesus Christ. For in His blood is life and His words bring life."

T.J. was beginning to understand. If he wanted to be more like Jesus he needed to make sure that what came out of his mouth would be the words that Jesus might speak if He were in his very shoes. T.J. turned to say something again to the angel, but the Word Angel had disappeared.

T.J. awoke to the calling of his mother's voice coming from downstairs.

"Time for dinner, T.J." she called.

T.J. threw off the covers and ran into the bathroom to check and see if his tongue was indeed black from the bad language he had been using. With a sigh of relief he smiled, for his tongue had not turned black.

"Coming mother," said T.J. as he raced downstairs with tears in his eyes.

"What's the matter dear?" mother asked bending over him.

"Oh mother," cried T.J. "I'm so sorry for the words I have spoken to you and to those on the playground. Will you forgive me?  I do love you and God so much and I'll never, never use bad words again."

"You are forgiven," smiled his mother.

Already T.J. could picture the recorded death words in heaven being erased and words of life and love taking their place on his tongue once again.

Words of life and beauty, teach me faith and duty *Beautiful words, wonderful words, wonderful words of life.*

-Wonderful Words of Life by P.P. Blise

*What lessons do we learn from the story of the Word Angel?*

*Are there dishonorable words you've been using that you need to confess to God, asking for His forgiveness?*

# The Third Commandment

EXODUS 20:7

## Do not take God's name in vain.

# Scripture Reading

*May the words of my mouth and the meditation of my heart be*
*pleasing in your sight, O Lord, my Rock and my Redeemer.*

PSALM 19:14

## KEY THOUGHT –

*If you care about God, handle His name with care.*

# The Guest of Honor

I s it time yet, is it Momma?" asked five year-old Abby as she tugged at her mother's pant leg.

"Not yet dear," said Mother, "but soon, very soon. We must be patient."

"I know," said Abby, "it's just that I'm so excited."

It had become a custom that every Sunday evening after the Yackley family attended church, they would end the Lord's Day with a family tea party to say thank you to their Guest of Honor.

"I'll get the napkins," cried Abby.

"I'll set out our tea cups," said Katie.

"I'll help mother," said Hannah.

All three girls looked forward to Sunday. It was a special time to sing about Jesus, learn wonderful Bible stories, and to be together as a family. Sunday had become the highlight of their week. Mother was making little finger foods for the children to munch on, as father set out chairs around the table on the back deck.

*Why was Sunday so important to this family?*

*What is so special about Sunday for you as a family?*

"How about now Mother?" asked Hannah as she wiggled and jumped with anticipation?

"Yes, now" said Mother.

The children squealed with excitement as they ran upstairs. You see, for those three girls, Sunday had become a time when they would bring out onto the back deck something that they had written or made throughout the week to show their thankfulness to the Guest of Honor. As the children came downstairs with their items, father had just finished putting out the chairs. All five of the chairs for the evening were very nice and comfortable, but there was a sixth chair that Mr. Yackley brought out that was far more special because it was reserved only for the Guest of Honor. The back and bottom of the chair had been hand woven from the finest textures and then covered with a dark purple velvet. Carved on one of the arms of the chair was a picture of a tender loving lamb sitting in a meadow. The other arm of the chair showed a mighty lion standing with authority. As often as the chair had been brought out on Sundays the children could not get over how beautiful it was. It was a chair that deserved to have a king sitting in it. And indeed it would.

As the family took their seats they all smiled when they saw the special chair at the head of the table. Together they bowed their heads and thanked God for Sundays. For Sunday had become the best day because it was the Guest of Honor's day. As they ate their little finger foods and drank their tea, they shared how God had protected, provided, and showed His love to them in so many different ways throughout the week. Finally Father looked at the girls and said, "Okay, who wants to go first?" The girls looked at each other with huge smiles. Finally Katie said, "I will begin if that is okay with you." The other two girls agreed. Katie slowly pulled a bag from under her chair and pulled out what was in it. There before them was a hand written poem. She had done some special art work around the corners and even sprinkled some cinnamon potpourri over the paper so it would smell good. Katie read her poem to her Guest of Honor and to her family. After she was done, she got out of her chair and placed the poem on the Guest of Honor's chair, and, with all the love she could hold inside her, bent down and said, "Thank you."

Hannah went next. She had crocheted a brightly colored cloth designed to polish and keep the Guest of Honor's chair from looking old and dusty. When Hannah was done, she too got

up from her chair, went over and placed the cloth on the Guest of Honor's chair. Closing her eyes she bent down and said, "I love you."

Finally it was Abby's turn. She had no special cloth, poem, or craft which she had made throughout the week. "This week," began Abby, "I decided instead of giving our Guest of Honor something I had made or written, that I would give him something else." Abby got up and went over to the chair, bent down and said, "I decided to give Jesus my life." As Abby's hands touched the arms of the chair she prayed, "Thank you, Jesus, for being the Guest of Honor in our home and in my heart." And all of Heaven rejoiced.

*Who is the Guest of Honor in your house?*

*Have you ever given your heart to Jesus like Abby did?*

*Why? Or why not?*

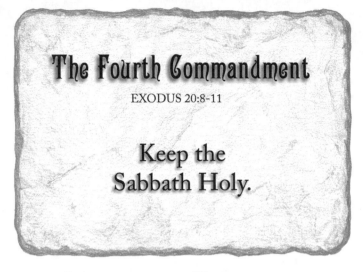

# The Fourth Commandment

EXODUS 20:8-11

## Keep the Sabbath Holy.

# Scripture Readings

*"Thus the heavens and the earth were completed in all their vast array. By the seventh day God had finished the work he had done; so on the seventh day he rested from all his work. And God blessed the seventh day and made it holy, because on it he rested from all the work of creating that he had done."*

GENESIS 2:1-3

*"I tell you that in the same way there will be more rejoicing in heaven over one sinner who repents than over ninety-nine righteous persons who do not need to repent."*

LUKE 15:7

## KEY THOUGHT –

*Remember the goodness and graciousness of God!*

# Heroic Moments

"Are we there yet?" asked Tony as he and his father rumbled down the expressway in their family mini-van. "Not yet," said Tony's dad, "it will be a few more minutes." Tony was so excited as he sat in the front seat on the passenger's side with his arms folded, and his elbows propped up on the door frame looking out the window at the landscape whizzing by.

"How about now, do you see it?" Tony asked, turning to his father.

"Almost," replied Tony's dad with a grin, keeping his eyes on the road as he turned onto the exit ramp. He knew how his son had been looking forward to this day for a long time. Tony looked down at the old glove in his lap and picked it up. It was very dirty and worn, having weathered many seasons, yet the soft leather pocket still had a lot of play in it. It had been his father's before, and this had made it all the more special when he received it last year on his tenth birthday.

"There it is," said Tony's dad, pointing to his right.

Tony looked up and saw the pennants flapping briskly in the wind and the huge scoreboard towering over the bleachers. They parked the car and began walking toward the stadium. Stopping at a souvenir stand, Tony's father bought him a Cubs hat. He knelt down, placed the blue cap on his head and smiled. Tony smiled back, and gave his dad a big hug. He remembered thinking how thankful he was to have a dad who took him to ball games.

Entering the stadium, they gave the usher their tickets and walked through the turnstyle. Immediately they were hit with the smells and sounds of people yelling, "hotdogs, popcorn, peanuts, Coke here." Tony's dad bought a program, a couple of hotdogs smothered in mustard, and some Cokes before sitting down in their front row bleacher seats out in center field. Tony's dad filled out the program's score sheet during batting practice, as Tony took out his baseball cards and looked through them. He stopped when he came to Willie Davis. He was his favorite player on the Cubs team. He played center field, the same position Tony played in Little League. Tony loved watching him run with his long graceful stride and dive, catching the ball just before it hit the ground. He was Tony's hero.

They stood for the National Anthem. As they took off their hats and placed their right hand across their hearts Tony felt his father put his arm around him as they sang together. Again they smiled at each other, their hearts filled to the brim with the love of a father for his son and a son for his father.

> **What does it mean to treat your mom and dad with honor and respect?**
>
> **What are some ways we can show honor to them?**

The umpire yelled, "Play ball!" As Willie came out to take his position, Tony's section cheered loudly, and Willie acknowledged the applause with a tip of his cap.

It was a very exciting game with the lead changing hands several times. In the eighth inning, the Cubs were down 8-5 and Willie Davis was up with two outs and the bases loaded. The count was 3 and 2 when Willie hit a knee high fast ball into the first row of the center field bleachers where it landed securely in Tony's glove. The crowd went wild, and as Willie rounded the bases, Tony thought to himself, I want to be just like him when I grow up.

In the ninth, the Mets loaded the bases with two outs, and their star player, Ron Johnson, hit a fly ball into the gap in right-center. Willie ran across the field at full speed and dove at the last second making a fantastic, shoestring, game-saving catch. The packed house rose in unison giving Willie a five minute standing ovation.

Afterwards, Tony and his father went down to the dugout to

see if they could get Tony's ball signed. The usher told them
that they would have to wait until they got changed and finished with their interviews. Well, they waited for what seemed
like an eternity until, finally, the players emerged. When Willie
came out, a mob of screaming fans surrounded him, pushing
Tony and his dad to the back. Tony began thinking exactly
what he would have him write while he waited. At last, Tony
was next in line. Willie had just finished with the person in
front of him, when a reporter came up and said that he wanted
to do a cover story, and he needed Willie right away. Well,
there was only Tony and about ten other people left, but Willie
turned to them and said that he had to leave. Tony held the

ball out to him and told him he was one of his biggest fans, and that he had caught his home run in the eighth, and how he played center field on his team and that he had waited for over an hour just to get his autograph. Tony looked at his hero with pleading eyes, but Willie only looked away and said, "Sorry kid, that's all for today," and walked away. Tony just stood there with his father's hand on his shoulder, watching him fade into the darkness.

"Ready to go champ?" asked his father, picking him up and placing him on top of his shoulders as they walked toward the car.

Left behind in a trash can lay a baseball and a stack of trading cards with Willie Davis's card torn in half lying on top. Tony knew that his real hero was taking him home.

— A special thanks to Chris Henley who had given me the idea for this particular commandment.

*Is your earthly father a heroic example to follow?*

*Why or Why not?*

*What special childhood memories do you have of you with your parents?*

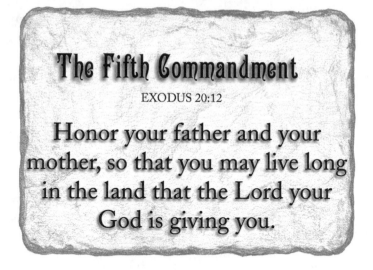

# The Fifth Commandment

EXODUS 20:12

Honor your father and your mother, so that you may live long in the land that the Lord your God is giving you.

# Scripture Readings

JOSHUA 3:14-4:7, 18-24

*How great is the love the Father has lavished on us, that we should be called children of God! And that is what you are!*

I JOHN 3:1

## KEY THOUGHT –

*Respect and appreciate the special things your parents do for you.*

# Showdown at Vulture Creek

he twins awoke in the morning to more than two feet of snow. Schools were closed for at least a day, which meant one thing for Danny and Charity— playing in the snow. As the twins stood in their pajamas looking out the front window, they could see a huge snow plow coming down the street pushing and spraying the snow high into the air making it look like a wave of white ocean water. Danny and Charity giggled as their breath frosted the window glass. Quickly, before the moisture could disappear, they wrote their names on the window and laid their hands on the cold window pane leaving a perfect palm print.

"Danny, Charity?" called their mother. "If you want to get out and play in the snow, then you'd better get into the kitchen or your breakfast is going to get cold."

"Okay, mom," they replied in unison, as they ran into the

kitchen and slipped into their chairs. Before them were two steaming hot waffles with delicious syrup dripping off the sides, a cold glass of milk, and some green grapes mom had just picked up at the grocery store the day before.

"Yum," they both said at the same time. Danny and Charity quickly ate and wiped off their sticky hands and mouths as mom laid out the mounds of clothes they would be wearing outside.

"Mom," said Danny in a puzzled tone, "it looks like you took all the clothes out of our closets. We are never going to be able to get all these clothes on and be able to run around and have fun in the snow."

"Now, now," replied mother. "You make sure you keep your coats buttoned and your gloves on. Even though the sun is shining, it is still very cold out there."

"We will," they said as they quickly put on their long johns, stocking caps, waterproof gloves and wool scarves. When they were finally dressed the twins looked like oversized parade balloons ready to float away.

"Mom, I can hardly move with all these clothes on," moaned Danny.

"Yeah," said Charity, "and I think I have to go to the bathroom."

"Oh, no," exclaimed Mom as she began the long process of undressing and then redressing Charity for the elements outside.

Finally, with shovels, buckets, and an ice cream scoop to make the perfect snow balls, they made their way outside. They looked more like stiff robots, than two kids ready to play in the snow.

"Hey," shouted Danny, "let's make a giant snowman!"

"Yeah," smiled Charity, "it will be the biggest one in the neighborhood."

They both began to scoop and pack a hand sized snowball and then began rolling it over the surface of the snow. The snowball began to get bigger and bigger and bigger, until together they could hardly move it.

"Hey, look at this?" said Charity, as she crawled up on the huge snowball. "I'm queen of the snow women."

"Yeah, right," mocked Danny, "more like queen of the snow drift," as he playfully pushed her off the mound of snow into a snow drift that cushioned her fall. Together they laughed and talked as they rolled several other snowballs to make the remainder of the snowman. Charity ran in the house to ask her mom if they could have a long carrot for the snowman's nose and some black buttons that mom kept in her sewing box underneath her bed for his jacket. Mom agreed and gave her what they needed. She also gave her a hat to place on the snowman for when they were finished.

"Mom, isn't this dad's hat?" asked Charity.

"Yes, but he doesn't wear it anymore. Besides, it's out of style, but it will be just right for your snowman. He'll be the best dressed snowman on the block!"

Charity gave her mom a big hug and ran back out to where her brother was. Suddenly, out of the corner of their eyes they could see Billy Murdock coming down the street pulling his bright red sled behind him.

"Uh-oh," they said at the same time, "here comes trouble."

Billy stopped in front of their house, looked at the snowman the twins were making, and let out a loud, devilish laugh.

"You call that a snowman?" That's terrible. Who taught you how to make a snowman? It looks more like a "snow monster!" Again, Billy let out a sinister laugh. "The only good thing about your "snow monster" is that by the end of the day it will be melted and it will be put out of its misery!"

"Very funny," said Danny as he picked up a snowball and was squaring up his body to throw it at Billy.

"Come on," said Billy, "give it your best shot. I bet your arm is so weak you can't even get it close to me, let alone hit me with it."

"Oh, yeah," Danny said with a cutting glare, as he began rearing back to throw a fast snowball.

"Hold on," yelled Charity. "Don't waste "our" good snow on someone who can't say anything nice. Besides this is "our" snowman and we are proud of it, so you are not invited over to see it. So be on your way." Charity moved her arms and hands urging him to move on.

"Fine," smirked Billy, "I was going sled riding over at Vulture Creek anyway. It will be more fun there, than to be with the both of you. In fact it would be more fun to be anywhere rather than with the two of you," and on his way he went.

Danny and Charity put the hat, eyes, mouth and scarf on their new snowman friend. "All we need now," said Danny "are some arms and we are finished." Finding some dead branches in their back yard, they gave their friend some arms and hands.

"There, finished," said Danny, as he clapped his gloves together with approval.

"Not yet," said Charity, "we still have one more thing to do."

"What's that?"

"We need to have our snowman protected from anyone who might want to harm him."

"What? Are you serious?" replied Danny.

"Yes," said Charity. "We need to have some snow angels protecting him."

Charity laid down in the snow and started to make a snow angel. "Like this," she said as she looked like she was doing jumping jacks in gym class.

Danny laid on his back and did the same thing on the opposite side of the snowman.

"There," she said, "finished. He's protected from both sides by God's beautiful angels."

Forgetting the time, they didn't even realize it was time for lunch until mom called out and told them that she had warm soup and some sandwiches ready for them at the kitchen table.

"Yum," they both said together as they ran to the house.

*What are some things you enjoy doing with your friends?*

*What might be the best thing to do when a "Billy Murdock" crosses your path?*

Billy Murdock was mad!

"How dare Danny and Charity talk to me that way," he said to himself in a huff as he tugged and pulled his red sled through the field toward Vulture Creek. "I should go back and push Danny down and throw a snow ball right in his face." Suddenly Billy had an idea. But it was not a good idea.

"Or maybe," he said out loud, "I'll sneak back right now and destroy their snowman, and take that silly hat they had on him and then go back to Vulture Creek and act like nothing happened." And that is exactly what Billy did. While Danny and Charity were enjoying their lunch, Billy came back and knocked over their snowman, broke the branches they made for arms and hands, ate the carrot, put the buttons in his pocket and put the hat on his head as he quickly ran on his way toward Vulture Creek.

When the twins looked outside they wanted to cry. Someone had ruined their snowman and had taken the buttons and hat they had used to dress him up. They also saw that their snow angels were trampled on and the broken branches laid all around. Charity began to cry.

"Who could do such a thing?" she sobbed. "Why would anyone do such a thing?"

"I'm not sure," replied Danny, "but I have a pretty good guess of who it might be." He noticed a trail of fresh footprints in the snow headed in the direction of the open field toward Vulture Creek.

Charity and Danny tried to repair their snowman, but it was no use. The excitement and joy that they first had, was now ruined by someone who was very mean and didn't respect the property of others. Danny looked at Charity.

"I know who it is, and I'm going to do something about it."

"What?" said Charity

Danny bent down and began to make snowballs with the ice cream scoop. But what Danny did next made Charity scared. Danny began to put rocks in the snowballs!

"What are you doing, Danny?"

"I'm going to Vulture Creek and I'm going to show Billy Murdock a thing or two," said Danny.

"What are you going to do with those snowballs with rocks in them?" she asked.

With a voice and look of anger, Danny said, "I'm going to throw them at Billy—I'm going to kill him!"

"You can't do that," she pleaded. "That's murder!"

"Oh, yeah, you just watch me." Danny loaded his pockets with the snowballs and headed in the direction of the footprints.

Charity ran to Danny and pleaded and begged him not to go. What he was going to do was wrong. It was not right, it was something God was against. But Danny wasn't listening.

"It's just a snowman," she pleaded, "we can always make another one."

"No, this time Billy's going to learn a hard lesson about keeping his mouth shut and not hurting or destroying something that doesn't belong to him." And then he added as he looked at the snowballs, "a rock hard lesson."

*What is Danny planning on doing when he finds Billy Murdock?*

*Is this the right thing to do?*

*Have you ever gotten mad at someone and wanted to hurt them?*

When Danny and Charity arrived at Vulture Creek, everyone was finished sledriding, and had gone home, except Billy Murdock. There on the top of the sled riding hill stood Billy with his red sled in his hands and the hat on his head he had stolen off the snowman. Danny shouted, "I know what you did Billy, and I'm going to kill you," as he began to run in Billy's direction. Billy could see the hatred in his eyes, and hear the anger in his voice. Billy began to panic. There was no place to hide and he was scared. So he began to run as fast as he could down the hill and at the last second belly flopped onto his sled. If he could sled ride all the way to the bottom he thought he might have a better chance of getting away. He knew, though, that it wouldn't be forever, because Danny and Charity knew where he lived.

Billy began to pick up speed, lots of speed. He was going faster on the sled than he had ever remembered. Suddenly, Billy remembered why they called the hill Vulture Creek. For there at the bottom of the hill was a creek. No one had ever sledded into it, but Billy had picked up so much speed from running down the hill before jumping on his sled that he was fastly approaching the creek. Billy let out a shrill scream as he broke through some dead branches and went plummeting down the rocky embankment where the creek laid below. The sled went one way as it hit a rock and Billy went another as he tumbled down the embankment smacking his head on a jagged rock before he broke the surface of the iced over creek and fell in. Suddenly, everything was quiet. Billy laid in the water unconscious with a three inch bloody gash above his right eye. Charity and Danny ran to the edge of the embankment and saw Billy laying in the water and his face covered with blood.

Suddenly, the threats of wanting to kill Billy seemed very wrong and frightening to Danny. The anger and determination Danny had to want to kill Billy now disappeared and an overwhelming concern for Billy flooded his soul. Quickly Danny and Charity worked their way down the steep embankment to where Billy lay.

"We've got to get him out of this water or he's going to freeze to death," they said in unison. Charity and Danny lifted Billy out of the water and managed to pull him over onto the snow covered embankment. Charity had several tissues in her pocket which she used to help stop the bleeding from Billy's forehead. Danny removed Billy's blood stained jacket, and then took off his own jacket and put it on Billy. Suddenly Billy's eyes opened and he asked where he was. He then realized that the two people helping him were Danny and Charity.

"Don't be scared," said Danny, "everything is going to be alright. We gotta get you out of these wet clothes and you'll need to get to a hospital to have them stitch up that nasty gash above your eye." Billy tried to say something, but Charity quieted him. "We are here for you," she whispered.

Tears appeared in Billy's eyes. "I'm so sorry," he said. "It was wrong of me to ruin your snowman and step on your snow angels. Will you ever forgive me?" Danny smiled and thought, "It's amazing how just minutes ago I wanted to kill Billy, but now I want to help save his life and love him like God would want me to do." "Sure we forgive you Billy. We are here for you; now let's get you home and into some warm clothes."

As they were working their way through the field toward home, Billy mumbled, "You two are the best snow angels a person could ever have. Thank you for protecting me and coming to my rescue. You saved my life. How could I ever repay you?"

Danny smiled as he unloaded from his pockets the snowballs that held rocks in them. "Hey, don't mention it," grinned Danny. "Maybe you can repay us by helping us build a new 'snow monster.' I think that's what you called it, wasn't it?"

Smiling, the three huddled together as they reached the crest of the hill where their homes could be seen in the distance.

*What important lessons do we learn from the story of Showdown at Vulture Creek?*

*In what ways could you show love to the "Billy Murdock's" in your life?*

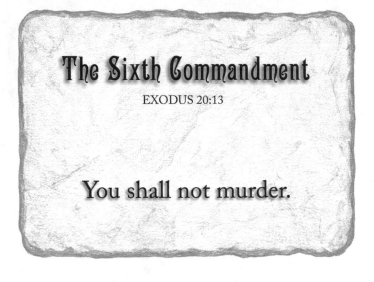

# The Sixth Commandment

EXODUS 20:13

## You shall not murder.

# Scripture Reading

*I have set before you life and death, blessing and curses.*
*Now choose life, so that you and your children may live and*
*that you may love the Lord your God, listen to His voice,*
*and hold fast to Him. For the Lord is your life. . .*

DEUTERONOMY 30:19-20

## KEY THOUGHT –

*Life is precious. Learn to take a stand against*
*anything that hurts the life or well-being of*
*others.*

# Faithful Unto Death

Zachary and Kelly watched the seagulls flying overhead as they walked out onto the sandy beach with their parents. It had been a great week together. As a family they had played in the ocean, gone out for pizza, made sand castles, and watched the sunset in the evening. Zachary and Kelly ran up ahead, chasing the waves back out into the ocean, while their mom and dad lagged behind holding hands and talking about the wonderful vacation they had as a family.

This was their last day at the beach and they wanted to make sure they got up early while the tide was low. The kids wanted to collect some seashells so they could take them back to school and use them for show and tell.

Each holding a plastic bucket, Zachary and Kelly began picking up seashells. Wide eyed with curiosity, they bent down again and again to examine what the ocean had washed up onto the shore. Some of the shells where very tiny, about the size of Kelly's pinky finger, while others were bigger than Zachary's fist. After finding a colorful or exotic shell, they would quickly run over to mom and dad and show them.

"Isn't it beautiful? Can we take this one home? Can we, Mom and Dad?" they would say jumping up and down.

"Yes," said Mom and Dad smiling.

"I think we might have a car load of seashells before we are done here," whispered Mom.

"Yeah, and a ton of sand to go with them," Dad replied with a playful grin.

"Wow," said Kelly, as she picked up a shell that was purple and pink in color. "I think I'll put this one on my night stand at home to remind me of God's creation and how much fun we've had this week."

Kelly glanced over at Zachary, who was now down on all fours looking at something in the sand. The water having lapped up onto the shore, looked foamy as it retreated back into the ocean.

"Look" he said. "Is that what I think it is?" Everyone came over to see what Zachary was looking at. There, half buried in the sand, was a shark's tooth that measured about one inch in length. It was pure black and pointed at the end.

"Wow," exclaimed their parents. "You sure don't find many of these around. You're fortunate to have one this size wash up on shore. By nine o'clock this morning, the tide would have washed it back out to sea, and it would have been gone forever."

Kelly asked, "Do you think it hurt the shark when he lost his tooth?"

"Maybe," said her mother. "He might have broken it off when he was eating something, or maybe this was his baby tooth and there was another tooth that needed to come through."

"You mean like the tooth I'm ready to lose?" With her tongue Kelly wiggled a tooth which was about ready to come out.
"Yes," smiled Mother, "you will eventually lose that tooth, and then a permanent tooth will come in."

The family continued to walk down the coast line, looking at the morning sunrise, smelling the salty sea air and savoring the memory of their vacation before they needed to load up and return home. Kelly and Zachary were running to another pile of shells that had washed ashore, when suddenly Kelly stopped.

"Yuck!" she exclaimed, wrinkling her nose. "What is that? It's gross!"

Zachary quickly ran over, "Wow! That's cool! Hey, look Mom, and Dad!" they both squealed.

Mom and Dad walked over and bent down. There on the sand were two angelfish that had washed ashore. The two angelfish were beautiful. Each one was almost gold in color with a little crimson red around their head and gill area.

"I wonder how they died," said Kelly as she bent closer to examine the color and texture of the two angelfish. Dad and Mom looked at each other and smiled. Dad began to share with the kids an old legendary story.

"When a male and female angelfish mate and become partners, they become partners for life. It has been said that when two angelfish love each other, nothing can separate them– not even death. They are very protective of each other and in many ways have given their hearts to one another. They do not want to harm their partner by swimming off with another fish, so when one angelfish dies, the other angelfish sinks to the bottom and dies too. I guess it's an expression of the fish's commitment and love to its partner."

"Kind of like you and Mom," said Zachary. "I mean, both of you love each other and are committed to each other till death, right?"

"Exactly," smiled Dad. "Your mother and I are partners for life, just like these two angelfish. Neither I nor your mother want to do anything to hurt our marriage and love for each other. And, like the angelfish, we are committed to one partner and only one."

Kelly smiled, "I know," she said. "That's why you're always holding hands and kissing."

"Yuck," winced Zachary. "That's gross!"

"I think it's kind of romantic," said Kelly as she threw her head back and rapidly blinked her eyes.

Dad continued, "God tells us in the Bible that we are to be loyal and committed to the one we marry. He tells us in the seventh commandment that we are not to commit adultery."

"What is that?" inquired Zachary. Kelly spoke up before mom or dad could speak.

"That means you're not supposed to cut down any adult trees, right mom?"

"Not exactly," smiled mother. "It means that we are to show respect for the opposite sex by keeping our thoughts and actions pure and by remembering to give our heart and body to our spouse and only our spouse.

Dad winked at Mom as if to say, "Well done."

"Dad, do you think Kelly and I will ever find someone special like you found Mom?"

Dad smiled. "We sure pray you do."

"Hey Mom," said Kelly, "do you think we could take these two angelfish and bury them somewhere?"

"Sure," replied Mom.

Together they moved further from the ocean and dug a hole deep enough to bury the fish so no one would disturb them. As they covered up the angelfish with sand, Kelly put her hands on her hips and said, "There—faithful unto death."

Dad smiled as he slipped his arm around his wife, "Yes," he said. "Faithful unto death."

*What important lessons do we learn about the loyalty of the angelfish and the seventh commandment?*

# The Seventh Commandment

EXODUS 20:14

## You shall not commit adultery.

# Scripture Readings

*May your fountain be blessed, and may you rejoice in the wife of your youth.*

PROVERBS 5:18

*But a man [or woman] who commits adultery lacks judgment; whoever does so destroys themselves.*

PROVERBS 6:32

*Husbands love your wives, just as Christ loved the church and gave himself up for her. . .without stain or wrinkle or any other blemish, but holy and blameless. . .*

EPHESIANS 5:25,27

## KEY THOUGHT —

*Keep your heart and mind pure and your actions will follow!*

# By Your Face it Shows

I t was the big day of the field trip. Matt and Allison had been looking forward to their fourth grade class going to the local chocolate factory ever since their teacher had told them. As the children got on the yellow bus to go to the factory, their teachers reminded them that they needed to stay together, mind their manners, and most importantly, there would be no sampling of any chocolate as they walked through the factory.

When they got to the chocolate factory and walked inside they immediately smelled the sweet aroma of chocolate. "Yum," said the children as they imagined what they might see just around the corner.

A man in charge of the factory greeted them with a warm smile and said, "Hello children, how many of you love chocolate?" Every hand went up as the children shouted "I do, I do!"

"We have white chocolate, milk chocolate, and dark chocolate here. We make chocolate bunnies, chocolate hearts, chocolate pretzels and much, much more. But our favorite here at the factory is a special train made out of all three kinds of chocolate." The man reached over on a table and showed everyone the bite size chocolate train.

"Wow," said the kids. "How can I get one of those?" said another child.

"Well," said the man smiling, "there might be a surprise at the end of the tour if we all listen and mind our manners." The children began to giggle and whisper to one another about what kind of surprise they might receive at the end of the tour.

"Who wants to take a trip through the chocolate factory?" asked the man.

Again every hand went up. "I do, I do!" Sure enough, as they rounded the corner they could see large containers of warm chocolate just waiting to be poured into different kinds of molds. As they made their way through the factory they saw workers putting plastic around the chocolate figures in order to keep them fresh. Others were putting chocolate into boxes to be sent out to the local grocery stores. Others were stirring the large containers of chocolate. Matt and Allison were so excited about seeing everything that they began to slip to the back of the group. "Allison," said Matt, "look at all this delicious chocolate. My mouth is so hungry for a piece."

"I know what you mean," said Allison.

As they were coming to the end of the field trip, the children came upon a large table where hundreds and hundreds of chocolate trains laid out to cool. "These trains that we've made today are very special," said the man. "These trains are not going to a local grocery store, but we are sending these trains to children in India and Russia who may never have had a chance to eat chocolate or may be too poor to buy any." The children just stared in amazement. The wheels on the train were white chocolate, the train itself was a light chocolate and the smoke stack was made from a dark chocolate. "By this time next week there are going to be some very happy children in India and Russia," said the man.

As the children were led into another room Matt and Allison lagged behind looking at all the trains before them. As they looked around they noticed there were several trains on the table that had broken when they came out of the mold. "I wonder what they will do with these?" asked Allison.

"Probably throw them away," said Matt. "Or maybe we could eat the broken ones and then they wouldn't have to worry about throwing them away." Allison agreed. Suddenly, Matt and Allison found themselves shoving chocolate into their mouths as fast as they could. "It will be our little secret," they said as they kept eating the parts of the train that laid before them.

Forgetting the time, Matt said in a panic, "We better catch up with the group or we're going to miss the bus." Dropping what they were doing, they quickly ran to the bus where the children were climbing aboard. Matt and Allison slipped to the back of the line acting like they had done nothing wrong. Up ahead they could see their teacher, Mrs. Walters, handing each child a box as they got on the bus. Matt and Allison smiled to themselves as they thought how great it would be to get somemore of that delicious chocolate which they had just sampled. As they came up to their teacher, she began to hand them the box of chocolate, but then stopped. She looked at their faces and bent down towards them. "Matt and Allison,"

she said, "I have one question for you. Have you taken any chocolate and eaten it on our field trip through the factory today?" Both hung their heads and admitted they had. "I thought so," she said, handing them a mirror. "Look at yourselves. By your face it shows. For there on their faces where chocolate marks and smudges. Their little secret was no longer a secret.

For Matt and Allison it was a long trip back on the bus. Everyone was laughing and enjoying their box of chocolate they received for minding their manners. Tears streamed down Matt's and Allison's faces. They sat together having received nothing but an awful tummy ache reminding them of the consequences that occur by taking something that doesn't belong to them.

*The trains were made to go some place special.*

*Where? Why?*

*What did Matt and Allison do that was wrong?*

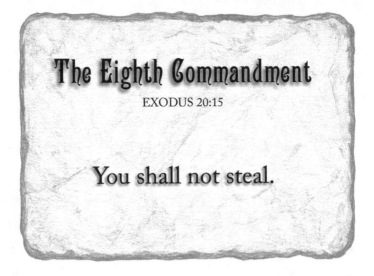

# The Eighth Commandment

EXODUS 20:15

## You shall not steal.

# Scripture Reading

*"He who has been stealing must steal no longer."*

EPHESIANS 4:28

## KEY THOUGHT –

*There are consequences to our sin!*

# No Trespassing

"He is so pretty," said Mollie as she gazed outside her window looking at one of Farmer Don's horses grazing in the pasture.

"I wish I was old enough to ride him and feel the wind whip across my face as we galloped through the meadow." Mollie sighed as she imagined being whisked away on the back of Indian Penny.

There were many horses in Farmer Don's pasture. But the one Mollie was drawn to the most was Indian Penny. Indian Penny got his name because he had a long black mane and coal black eyes, just like the Indians pictured in the history books she read. His coat was a beautiful copper color that glistened like a shining penny when the sunshine hit his body just the right way.

Mollie loved living next to Farmer Don. He was a wonderful

man, and when he was outside, which was most of the time, she was always allowed to come over. Almost every day after school she would find him somewhere on the farm in his blue jean overalls with a red handkerchief peeking out of his back pocket. His laugh was contagious and his smile could warm the heart of any child. But lately, something was troubling Farmer Don. It seemed that there were prowlers coming onto his farm land in the middle of the night trying to stir up trouble. For weeks now he could hardly sleep, and his cattle, sheep, and horses were restless as well.

One day after school Mollie saw Farmer Don out by the horse pasture nailing something up to the wooden fence post.

"What are ya doing Farmer Don?" asked Mollie.

Startled by Mollie's voice, he jumped, causing Mollie to giggle.

"Oh, you scared me Mollie," he said. "I was just putting up these signs around the farm to tell uninvited folks to stay away and to keep out. Farmer Don moved away for Mollie to read what he had nailed up. NO TRESPASSING—KEEP OUT!

"Does that include me?" inquired Mollie with a slight grin on her face knowing what Farmer Don would say.

"Certainly not, child," he said, "but it does mean that if you want to pet Indian Penny you must be with me. We cannot afford to lose any of our horses through this gate here. So if you want to pet him or feed him, come knock on my door and we will walk out together. Is that a deal little sweetheart?" He knelt down beside her and held out his hand.

"That's a deal," she said as they shook hands and then hugged.

> **Why was Farmer Don putting a sign up that read...**
> **NO TRESPASSING KEEP OUT!**

Over the next week Mollie would come over to Farmer Don's house after school and ask if they could go out together to pet Indian Penny. Together, hand in hand, they would walk to the horse gate, unlatch it and then close it behind them, so that the horses would not get out. Farmer Don would bring various brushes and picks to smooth out Indian Penny's coat and to pick out any rocks or clumps of dirt that might be in his horseshoes.

Every time they were ready to leave, Farmer Don would pick Mollie up and place her on the back of Indian Penny. Her eyes would grow wide with excitement as she stroked Indian Penny's mane and head.

"Someday," said Farmer Don, "you will be old enough to ride him by yourself."

"Yeah," said Mollie with a smile, "someday."

Closing the gate behind them, Mollie again saw the sign Farmer Don had nailed to the wooden fence post. NO TRES-PASSING—KEEP OUT!

It was Saturday and Mollie had finished doing her chores when her mother asked her to go out into the garden to pick some fresh carrots for the evening meal. Mollie skipped out to the garden and began to pull some of the best looking carrots you have ever seen. As she pulled them, she glanced up to see Indian Penny standing by himself, looking her way. "Hello," she shouted as she waved to him. Indian Penny returned the greeting with a loud and joyful neigh.

Mollie brought the carrots inside and placed them at the sink where they could be washed off, and prepared for dinner.

"Why don't you take a few of these over to your friend," said mother.

Mollie jumped up and down with glee as she took six carrots from the top of the pile. Mollie thanked her mother and raced out the door toward Farmer Don's house. She couldn't remember ever running so fast in her life. Standing on his front porch, Mollie knocked several times, but no one answered.

"Maybe he's in the barn," she thought as she quickly ran around to the side of the barn. But inside there was no one, just a few chickens pecking at the feed that had been tossed to them that morning.

"He must be around here somewhere," thought Mollie.

She looked over by where the cows had gathered, and over by where the pigs feed, but Farmer Don could not be found. Mollie grew sad as she sat on a wooden stump outside of the barn.

"What am I going to do with these carrots if I can't give them to Indian Penny?" thought Mollie. Then she had an idea. She could quickly go into the fenced area where Indian Penny was, feed him the carrots, and then quickly leave. Farmer Don wouldn't

even know. Besides she knew how to open and close the gate. She had been with him dozens of times to see how it was done.

Quickly she got up and ran towards the gate where Indian Penny stood. She hesitated in unlocking the gate when she saw the sign. NO TRESPASSING-KEEP OUT! She knew she had made a deal with Farmer Don about not going inside the pasture without him, but it would only be for a moment. Something inside her told her that she had made a promise, that she was to keep her word. "If you can't stand on your word, then you have nothing to stand on," her dad had told her.

She was startled when she heard Indian Penny neigh again. Smiling at him she quickly forgot her promise and unlatched the fence gate. Mollie gave all six carrots to Indian Penny and he munched them up one by one. To show his appreciation, he rubbed his head against Mollie's face. She stood there with her friend talking and stroking his copper coat and mane again and again. Suddenly Mollie heard the voice of her mother calling her to come home for dinner. Mollie quickly kissed Indian Penny good-bye on his forehead and raced toward the fence gate. Without thinking, she closed the gate, but did not latch it securely. Mollie ran home and enjoyed a delicious evening dinner and the carrots she had picked from the garden.

*What did Mollie do that was disobedient?*

*Have you ever done something that you knew was wrong?*

Sometime during the night, the horses became restless, apparently spooked by something out in the fields. No one knows for sure what it was, but it caused the horses to inch closer and closer to the gate which had not been securely latched. One of the horses eventually got so close to the gate that he actually rubbed up against it, causing it to swing open.

Frightened, the horses charged toward the open gate and broke into a wild gallop. Some went into the field across the road, some went into the woods and some went and stood quietly over near the barn. The horses were out and running everywhere.

Farmer Don was awakened by the sound of the horses. As he looked out his window he was shocked to see his horses running everywhere. "Someone had let them out," thought Farmer Don. "Who would do such a thing?" It would be a long evening for Farmer Don.

The next morning Mollie awoke, having no idea what had happened during the night. She looked outside and saw all the horses in the pasture as usual. But something was different. There in the pasture laid Indian Penny. He looked sad, he looked hurt. "What has happened to my friend?" she thought. "Who would want to hurt such a lovely creature as him?" Quickly she dressed and ran over to Farmer Don's. She found him by the horse gate. "What's wrong with Indian Penny?" she asked.

"All the horses got out last night. They somehow got out through this gate." Farmer Don knelt to examine it one more time. "Either someone let them out, or this gate was not latched properly the last time it was closed."

Mollie felt sick. She knew that it was her. She remembered quickly closing the gate, but forgetting to securely latch it.

"We think it was those prowlers that have been causing the horses and cattle to become restless," said Farmer Don. "I guess some people don't pay attention to signs like this," he said and pointed to the sign. NO TRESPASSING—KEEP OUT! Mollie wanted to cry. This was all her fault. She was the one to blame.

"And to make things worse," said Farmer Don, "Indian Penny

ran through a briar patch and scraped up his copper coat. He was bleeding pretty bad last night after we brought him back. He was badly hurt, but he'll be okay in a few weeks. It's going to take some time for those wounds to heal. Some will leave a permanent scar."

Mollie began to cry. Tears streamed down her face. Her heart was sad and she knew that she could not lie. She must tell the truth about what really happened. She knew she would get in trouble for telling the truth, but she knew for sure she'd get in trouble for telling a lie.

As Mollie looked over at Indian Penny, she knew that it would take years for his scars to fade, and it would take years for the scars of her disobedience to fade away as well. The truth must be told, she thought. So taking a deep breath, Mollie looked at Farmer Don and said, "Farmer Don, I have something to tell you."

Mollie learned a valuable lesson that day about telling the truth, and like Farmer Don said, "It's going to take some time for those wounds to heal." Telling the truth, though, has a way of making them fade away.

*What lessons can we learn about telling the truth and being honest rather than lying?*

  Carved In Stone

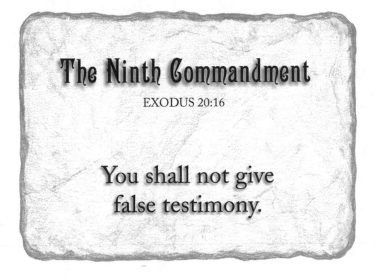

# The Ninth Commandment

EXODUS 20:16

## You shall not give false testimony.

# Scripture Reading

*Therefore each of you must put off falsehood and speak truthfully to his neighbor, for we are all members of one body.*

EPHESIANS 4:25

## KEY THOUGHT –

*A person who often tells lies, lives lies.*

# God Has His Reasons

The moment Grace was born she was a picture of beauty. Her hair was dark black and her eyes were a rich dark chocolate color which caused people to take a second glance and remark how beautiful she was. But as Grace got older she began to notice that other children her age had different colored eyes and hair. Some of the kids had ocean blue eyes and sandy blonde hair, while other children had emerald green eyes and light brown hair. Oh, how she longed to look like them.

One day Grace told her mother. "I want to have blue eyes like Jessica and blond hair like Kelly's, I'm tired of having brown eyes and black hair."

Grace's parents explained to her that God made her this way. That she was created by God and that He had something very special planned for her life. "You just wait and see," they would tell her, "God has His reasons. For He made you uniquely for Him."

As often as her parents would tell her how special and beautiful she was, Grace longed for the day when she could have blue eyes instead of brown and blonde hair instead of black.

"If only God would make me like my friends, she would say, I would be the happiest girl in the world." Lovingly, her parents again would smile and say," God has His reasons, you just wait and see."

One night when Grace was seven, she sat on her bed and looked into the full length mirror that was across the room. She did not like the way she looked at all. She was very sad.

"Dear Jesus," she said, "I want to be like the other boys and girls who have beautiful blue and green eyes and have hair that is brown or blonde. And Jesus, as I go to sleep tonight would you please turn my eyes blue and my hair blonde. I promise if you grant this one prayer, I will never, never, never ask you for another thing my entire life, if you will do this simple thing for me. Amen."

*Why was Grace so sad?*

Grace could hardly sleep that night. She tossed and turned, looking forward to morning when she would wake up and see the new her. Bright and early just as the sun was creeping up over the window sill and into her bedroom, she threw off the covers and ran to her mirror. Immediately, Grace began to cry. God had not changed her eyes or her hair at all! They were still the same as they were when she had gone to bed.

Grace's mother heard her crying and came into the room.

"Grace," said her mother. "What is it?"

"I don't want to have brown eyes and black hair, I want to be like the other kids at school."

Grace's mom brought her close and whispered in her ear, that God loved her and reminded her again that God has His reasons. She explained to Grace that her wanting something that someone else had, was not right, and that the Bible calls that coveting.

"What is coveting?" Grace asked.

"Well," replied her mother, "coveting is when you want to have different colored eyes and hair because someone else has them, and you think that by having these things it will make you happier. But God did not intend for you to have these things. As a result, you make God sad because you are not willing to be thankful and happy with what He has already given you. God wants us to be thankful for what He has given us, because what He has given us He will use for His good purpose in our life."

Grace wiped the tears away and together they prayed and thanked God for the way God had created her. Again Grace's

mother reassured her, "God made you uniquely special for His reasons, you just wait and see."

When Grace was fourteen years old, a missionary came to her church. She showed slides of great places all around the world where people were going and telling others about Jesus Christ. Grace saw people in those slides that had brown eyes and dark black hair just like hers and she wondered if one day God would have her be a missionary somewhere in the world. When Grace left the church that day she shook hands with the missionary.

"My, my," said the missionary, "you have beautiful eyes and hair." The missionary handed her a brochure as she walked out the door. As Grace got in the car and sat in the back seat she looked at the brochure. There on the front was a girl that looked just like her along with the words, "Come Home To India!"

Grace's mother touched her shoulder and smiled. "Remember, darling, God's got His reasons why He made you the way you are."

Throughout high school Grace wasn't so concerned about her hair and her eyes. Though she found herself from time to time looking at someone who had lighter eyes or hair, she kept in mind the words of her mother that God had made her as she was for a very special reason.

> *Why do you think Grace's mother kept saying,*
> *"God has His reasons?"*

Shortly after high school graduation, Grace was asked to attend a large college away from her home and her parents. As she was packing up her things for college, she came across a crumbled up brochure that had been pushed to the very back of her junk drawer. Unfolding it, she smiled as she saw the picture of the beautiful girl on the front cover with the words, "Come Home To India."

Grace wondered if this was the special reason for why God made her this way. Grace prayed that day that if God wanted her to one day go to India to serve Him, that He would make it clear and bring people into her life to help her understand what it was like to live in India.

No sooner had Grace arrived at her college dorm room when she opened the door to go in and saw her roommate for the first time. Grace's jaw dropped and her eyes welled up with tears. For there unpacking was the very girl that was in the brochure that she had saved for many years.

Grace knew that God truly had His reasons all along and she wouldn't trade her dark brown eyes nor her dark black hair for anything in the entire world. Grace knew that one day she would be serving as a missionary in India and it would be just like the brochure said... Come Home to India.

Grace stopped, knelt down and thanked the Lord for making her so special– for truly God has His reasons.

*What lessons can we learn about coveting that Grace had to learn?*

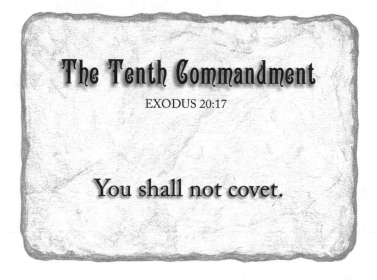

# The Tenth Commandment

EXODUS 20:17

## You shall not covet.

# Scripture Readings

*Keep your lives free from the love of money
and be content with what you have...*

HEBREWS 13:5

*Be on your guard against all kinds of greed; a man's life does not
consist in the abundance of his possessions.*

LUKE 12:15

## KEY THOUGHT –

*The values of a Christian do not depend on
what he/she has, what he/she wears or how
he/she might look. Our value is based on who
we are in the eyes of our Savior.*

Finish Line Ministries was founded in 1992 with the purpose of "Calling the church worldwide to biblical obedience." Finish Line Ministries is an interdenominational revival ministry which travels the country and the world, preaching and teaching the truths of God's Word. The Lord has used this preaching to change thousands of lives, as individuals have either found salvation in Jesus Christ, or recommitted themselves to a closer walk with the Savior.

Finish Line Ministries provides a wide variety of gifted speakers and resources in helping people establish a strong spiritual foundation with God.

For future bookings and speaking engagements, call or write:

Finish Line Ministries
PO Box 14343
Columbus, OH 43214-0343

614-538-6077

Email: flm@finishlineministries.org.
Website: www.finishlineministries.org.

About the illustrator:

Known for her breathtaking colored pencil portraits and still-lifes, Sharon Frank Mazgaj's illustrations are an expansion of her creative abilities. Sharon Frank Mazgaj delights the reader with her life-like illustrations which capture the theme and vividly depict the character in each story.

Sharon Frank Mazgaj received her BFA degree in Graphic Design from the University of Akron. She has worked professionally as an art teacher and in the advertising field.

Sharon has received numerous awards for her colored pencil works, and is an active member of the Colored Pencil Society of America (CPSA).

Sharon, her husband, and their three children reside in Green, Ohio.